FULANI

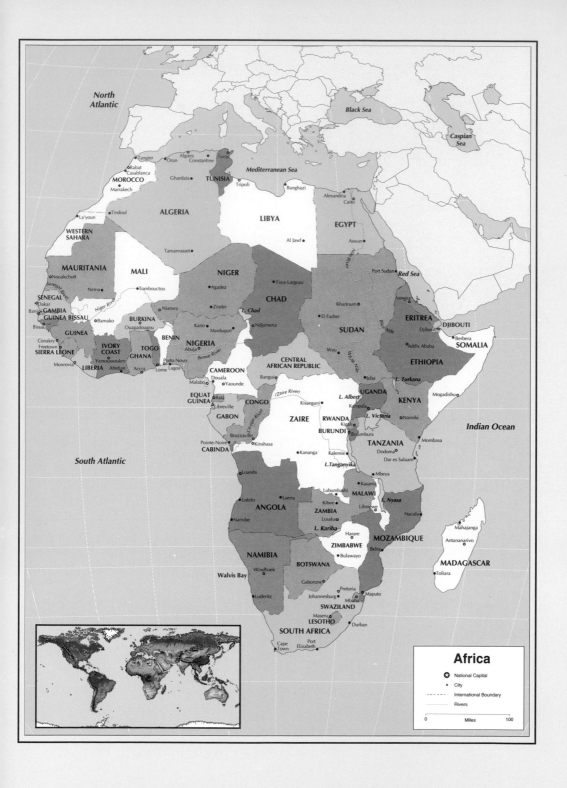

North
Atlantic

Black Sea

Caspian
Sea

Tangier
Rabat
Casablanca
MOROCCO
Marrakech
Ghardaia
Algiers
Constantine
TUNISIA
Tunis
Mediterranean Sea
Tripoli
Banghazi
Alexandria
Cairo

La'youn
Tindouf
WESTERN
SAHARA

ALGERIA

LIBYA

EGYPT

Aswan

MAURITANIA
Nouakchott
Nema

MALI

NIGER

Faya-Largeau

Port Sudan
Red Sea

Tombouctou
Agadez

CHAD

Khartoum

Asmara
ERITREA
DJIBOUTI

Niamey
Zinder
L. Chad

SENEGAL
Dakar
GAMBIA
Banjul
GUINEA BISSAU
Bissau
GUINEA
Conakry
Freetown
SIERRA LEONE
Monrovia
LIBERIA

Bamako
Ouagadougou
BURKINA
BENIN

Kano
Maiduguri
Ndjamena

El Fasher

SUDAN

Wau

Blue Nile
White Nile

Djibouti
Addis Ababa
Berbera
SOMALIA

ETHIOPIA

Mogadishu

IVORY
COAST
Yamoussoukro
GHANA
Abidjan
TOGO
Accra
Porto Novo
Lome Lagos
NIGERIA
Abuja
Benue River

CAMEROON
Douala
Yaounde

CENTRAL
AFRICAN REPUBLIC

Bangui

Juba

L. Turkana

EQUAT.
GUINEA
Bata
Libreville
CONGO
GABON

(Zaire River)
Kisangani

ZAIRE

L. Albert
UGANDA
Kampala
Kigali
RWANDA
BURUNDI
Bujumbura

L. Victoria
Nairobi
KENYA

Mombasa

Indian Ocean

South Atlantic

Pointe-Noire
CABINDA
Brazzaville
Kinshasa

Luanda

Kananga

Kalemie

L.Tanganyika

TANZANIA
Dodoma
Dar es Salaam

Mbeya

Kasama

Lobito
Luena
Lubumbashi
Kitwe
Lusaka
ZAMBIA
L. Kariba
MALAWI
Lilongwe
L. Nyasa
Nacala

Namibe
ANGOLA

Harare

NAMIBIA
Windhoek

BOTSWANA
Gaborone

ZIMBABWE
Bulawayo

Beira
MOZAMBIQUE

Mahajanga

Antananarivo

MADAGASCAR
Toliara

Walvis Bay

Luderitz

Johannesburg
Pretoria
Maputo
Mbabane
SWAZILAND
Maseru
LESOTHO
SOUTH AFRICA
Durban

Cape
Town
Port
Elizabeth

Africa

- ⊗ National Capital
- • City
- - - International Boundary
- — Rivers

0   Miles   100

The Heritage Library of African Peoples

FULANI

Pat I. Ndukwe, Ph.D.

THE ROSEN PUBLISHING GROUP, INC.
NEW YORK

Published in 1996 by The Rosen Publishing Group, Inc.
29 East 21st Street, New York, NY 10010

First Edition

Manufactured in the United States of America

Library of Congress Cataloging-in-Publication Data

Ndukwe, Pat I. (Pat Ikechukwu)
    Fulani / Pat I. Ndukwe. — 1st ed.
      p.   cm. — (The heritage library of African peoples)
    Includes bibliographical references and index.
    Summary: Describes the history, traditions, culture, and religion
  of the Fulani, who held political, religious, and military power
  over parts of western Africa for several centuries and still live in
  many countries there.
    ISBN 0-8239-1982-X
    1. Fula (African people)—Juvenile literature.   [1. Fula (African
  people)]   I. Title.   II. Series.
  DT474.6.F84N38   1995
  966'.00496322—dc20   95-287
                                                            CIP
                                                            AC

Contents

INTRODUCTION

THERE IS EVERY REASON FOR US TO KNOW something about Africa and to understand its past and the way of life of its peoples. Africa is a rich continent that has for centuries provided the world with art, culture, labor, wealth, and natural resources. It has vast mineral deposits, fossil fuels, and commercial crops.

But perhaps most important is the fact that fossil evidence indicates that human beings originated in Africa. The earliest traces of human beings and their tools are almost two million years old. Their descendants have migrated throughout the world. To be human is to be of African descent.

The experiences of the peoples who stayed in Africa are as rich and as diverse as of those who established themselves elsewhere. This series of books describes their environment, their modes of subsistence, their relationships, and their customs and beliefs. The books present the variety of languages, histories, cultures, and religions that are to be found on the African continent. They demonstrate the historical linkages between African peoples and the way contemporary Africa has been affected by European colonial rule.

Africa is large, complex, and diverse. It encompasses an area of more than 11,700,000 square miles. The United States, Europe, and India could fit easily into it. The sheer size is an indication of the continent's great variety in geography, terrain, climate, flora, fauna, peoples, languages, and cultures.

Much of contemporary Africa has been shaped by European colonial rule, industrialization, urbanization, and the demands of a world economic system. For more than seventy years, large regions of Africa were ruled by Great Britain, France, Belgium, Portugal, and Spain. African peoples from various ethnic, linguistic, and cultural backgrounds were brought together to form colonial states.

For decades Africans struggled to gain their independence. It was not until after World War II that the colonial territories become independent African states. Today, almost all of Africa is ruled by Africans. Large numbers of Africans live in modern cities. Rural Africa is also being transformed, and yet its people still engage in many of their customs and beliefs.

Contemporary circumstances and natural events have not always been kind to ordinary Africans. Today, however, new popular social movements and technological innovations pose great promise for future development.

George C. Bond Ph.D., Director
Institute of African Studies
Columbia University, New York

Today the Fulani, especially those that remain nomadic, have to strike compromises between tradition and modernity. These Fulani teenagers from Côte d'Ivoire clearly enjoy contemporary music.

chapter

1

THE PEOPLE AND THEIR LAND

THE FULANI REPRESENT A REMARKABLE diversity of habitation, culture, ethnic composition, and lifestyle. Further, for several centuries they maintained political, religious, and military power over several parts of western Africa.

The Fulani are very widely scattered all over the vast West African savanna of wooded grasslands, from Senegambia in the west to Chad and the western Sudan in the east, and Cameroon in the southeast. The largest concentrations of Fulani are in Senegambia, which includes Senegal and Gambia; the Fouta Jalon Highlands of Guinea; the upper and middle portions of the Republic of Niger; the northern region of Nigeria, particularly in Sokoto, Kebbi, Katsina, Kano, Jigawa, Borno, Yobe, Bauchi,

Through much of West and Central Africa, the Fulani are found both in settled populations, such as this Fulani village in Mali (top), and as nomads who move with their cattle herds (below).

and Plateau States; the Adamawa Highlands
spanning Nigeria and Cameroon; and the northern parts of Cameroon. Fulani are also found in
substantial numbers in Burkina Faso, Chad,
Mali, and Côte d'Ivoire.

The Fulani are referred to by various names.
The Hausa term *Fulani* is the most widely used.
The Wolof term *Peul* was adopted by the French.
The Kanuri call them *Felaata*, and the Germans
refer to them as *Fulbe* (singular *Pulo*). The
Fulani also refer to themselves generally as
Fulbe. However, they recognize two broad categories of Fulbe: the *Bororo* or Cattle Fulani;
and the *Toroobe* or Town Fulani, sometimes also
called *Fulani siire*, or, by the Hausa, *Fulanin gida*
or Home Fulani.

The Fulani call their language Fulfulde (or,
depending on the area, Pular, Peul, Fula, or
Ful). It belongs to the West Atlantic branch of
the great Niger-Congo language family. Because
of the wide geographical distribution of its
speakers, Fulfulde is spoken in many different
dialects. Apart from a few grammatical differences, the major differences usually occur in
vocabularies that have been adapted from the
dominant language of the different regions.
Most Fulani find it necessary, at least for commercial reasons, to speak the dominant language
of the area in which they live. In addition, they
may learn one or more of the area's minority

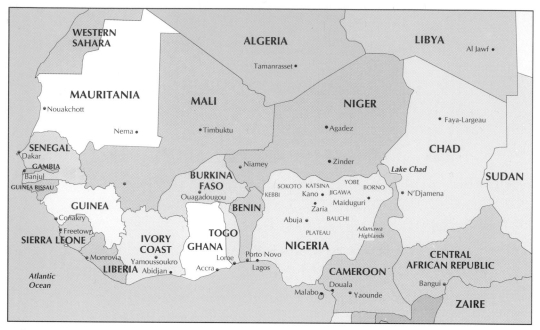

The Fulani are widely distributed from Senegal in the west to the Sudan in the east.

languages. With the increasing pressure of Western education, it is also fairly common for Fulani to speak English, French, and Portuguese.

Traditionally, the Fulani are a pastoral or cattle-raising people. Some Fulani are pure pastoralists and nomadic, whereas others are either completely or partially settled, mixing farming with pastoralism to varying degrees.

For pastoral Fulani, their whole lives revolve around their cattle. Their subsistence and wealth come entirely from their herds of cattle supplemented occasionally with sheep, goats, and camels. Some Fulani groups such as the

12

The Bororo, nomadic Fulani, are known for their elaborate body arts.
This young woman in the Central African Republic has many tattoos

The Bororo eat their cattle only on ceremonial occasions. This Fulani archer can obtain meat by shooting small animals.

Uda'en of northern Nigeria and Niger have no cattle but exist solely on flocks of sheep; however, such groups are extremely rare.

The pastoral Fulani live on dairy products. Surpluses are sold to buy grain and other food items. Meat is eaten only on ceremonial occasions. The attachment of the pastoral Fulani to their cattle is legendary; a cow is sold only when there is an overriding need for cash.

Pastoral Fulani practice transhumance, that is, the seasonal movement of livestock from one region to another in response to such factors as the availability of water, the presence of cattle diseases, and the availability of ready markets for business transactions.

A good number of Fulani are of the settled type. Some of the better-known settled Fulani groups include the Toucouleurs of Senegal, the Khassonke of Niger Republic, and the Hausa–Fulani of Nigeria. However, traditions still link the settled Fulani with their pastoral cousins.

The partially settled Fulani combine cattle ownership with crop farming. Cattle-owning is regarded as the more important of the two. Fulani generally become partially settled as a result of cattle loss from disease or some sudden disaster that forces them to turn reluctantly to farming. This state is usually transitional. If the cattle herd is somehow replenished, the Fulani return to pastoral life. If the loss persists, however, the group becomes absorbed by the surrounding agricultural communities.

Of the three categories of Fulani, the pastoralists have maintained their traditional cultural practices and values in their most pristine form. For that reason, discussion of Fulani cultural and social life concentrates on the pastoralists.▲

chapter

2

HISTORY AND
TRADITIONS

THE FULANI ARE ONE OF THE MOST NUMEROUS peoples of West Africa. Experts estimate the number at about ten million. In addition, they have had a significant impact on the whole subregion.

The origins of the Fulani, like those of many West African peoples, are basically unknown. European scholars of the late 19th and early 20th centuries believed that their origins began in places as far-flung as the Near East, northern Africa, and Ethiopia.

The Fulani themselves have their own beliefs about their origins. The most commonly held myth refers to the marriage of an Arab Muslim called Ukuba to an African woman from Fouta Toro. The marriage was blessed with four sons. The eldest of these sons showed early, through various signs, that he was destined for great

A mother and children at a Fulani camp in Côte d'Ivoire. The woman wears large amber beads.

things. For example, from infancy he spoke in an incomprehensible language that later developed into Fulfulde, the Fulani language. In one version of the myth, the eldest son and his brothers founded the four major Fulani branches. A variant of this version has the eldest son, Musa, founding the Toroobe or town Fulani, while the other brothers founded various branches of the Bororo or cattle Fulani. In another less popular version, the eldest son single-handedly founded the entire Fulani race while his brothers brought forth various (unspecified) African peoples.

Pastoral Fulani have their own exclusive myth of origin. The most common version states that the first Cattle Fulani was expelled from his settled clan for unstated reasons. After wandering the wilderness and enduring indescribable hardships, he happened on a water spirit by a

lake who promised him untold wealth and influence if he obeyed the spirit's orders. In one version he was required to water all the wild animals in turn until he was sent cattle as a reward
for his efforts. In another version he was simply
asked to wait patiently until the future source of
his wealth showed up. Cattle appeared from
nowhere, and the water spirit required him always to light a fire at dusk for them; otherwise
they would revert to their wild state and he
would lose them. This myth was supposed to
account for the source of the nomadic
pastoralists' wealth in cattle, and to explain why
the Town Fulani and the Cattle Fulani are not
always on the best of terms.

There is reason to believe that the Fulani may
have originated from the Fouta Toro in
Senegambia. Linguistic evidence shows that
Fulfulde is related to Wolof and Serer, two other
languages spoken in the same area. Such evidence often suggests a long historical relationship and a common source for both the languages and their speakers. The issue of Fulani
origins remains far from settled.

▼ FULANI MIGRATIONS ▼

If the Fulani did originate in the Fouta Toro
in Senegambia, their movement to the other
parts of West Africa must have been eastward. It
is not clear at what periods, or how, or in what

stages the various migrations took place. It is clear, though, that by the 18th and early 19th centuries, when the various Fulani-inspired Muslim holy wars or *jihads* were fought in parts of West Africa, substantial Fulani minorities already lived in those areas.

It is fairly certain that the movements eastward were lead by the pastoral Fulani. The practice of transhumance makes it necessary to adjust to changing ecological conditions by moving to new locations. Pastoral Fulani are also known to have moved whenever conditions became too hostile to be tolerated—deteriorating weather conditions, disease, and tax exploitation, to name a few. Whatever the cause for movement, the pastoral Fulani have sometimes moved on even as settled types remained.

Fulani holy men (Muslim scholars who also functioned as missionaries) also played a role in unifying and even furthering these migrations. In the course of their missionary journeys to spread Islam they succeeded in raising the political and religious consciousness of the scattered Fulani communities. Sometimes they even promoted uprisings against non-Muslim powers and had to flee with their followers into remote regions of the various empires and kingdoms they challenged. These were some of the basic characteristics of the various *jihads* that led to Fulani dominance in some parts of West Africa.▲

The life of nomadic Fulani centers on their herds, and they have few other material possessions. While men control the cattle (top), women's possessions chiefly consist of calabashes and other household utensils, which are placed on platforms when the group makes camp (bottom).

chapter

3

SOCIAL LIFE AND CUSTOMS

PASTORAL FULANI DO NOT BUILD COMPLEX social organizations. Because they are always on the move, every aspect of their existence has been organized to ensure maximum simplicity and efficiency.

As in every other human community, the basic unit of Fulani social and economic organization is the family. There are two kinds of Fulani family, simple and compound. The simple family is made up of the male head of the family, his wife, and their children. The compound family is composed of the male head, two or more wives, and their children. Usually there is no limit to the size of the family; the Fulani believe that the more children they have (especially males), the better it is for looking after the herd.

The Fulani family tries to function as an independent and self-sustaining unit, since nomads rarely move in groups of more than one family. Every family unit thus has to be self-sufficient, relying on themselves and their animals for survival.

▼ THE FAMILY AND THE HERD ▼

The relationship between family and herd is therefore necessarily symbiotic; that is, they are dependent on each other. The family unit not only is supported by its cattle, but for all intents and purposes exists for the sake of the cattle. The status of the family, especially of its head, is determined largely by the size and well-being of its cattle, just as the more a man knows about cattle-herding, the greater his respect in the community. It is no exaggeration to say that the loss of cattle is felt as keenly as the loss of family members. Only old and out-of-work bulls are killed or sold when this becomes necessary. It is considered a mark of a man's high regard for his bride if he offers a young bull as part of the bridewealth.

The closeness the Fulani feel with their cattle is reflected by the fact that they can easily identify each member of the herd and even have pet names for them. Their length of stay at any location is determined by how suitable it is for the cattle and, to a far lesser extent, for the family. A family without cattle ceases, in pastoral Fulani terms, to exist.

Fulani women, whether settled in towns or nomadic, take care of the household. This young woman carries a calabash container on her head. Included in her jewelry are silver coins dangling on her forehead and several kinds of expensive glass beads, which have been traded in Africa for many centuries. For nomadic people jewelry is a light and convenient way of storing wealth. In times of drought jewelry can be sold for cash.

▼ DIVISION OF WORK ▼

Just as the importance of a family unit or household is determined by the size and health of its herd, the roles of family members are defined in relation to the herd. Division of labor is strict between males and females. Men look after the cattle, and women are in charge of the milk and milk products such as butter. Males are not involved with household chores such as the preparation of meals, cleaning and decorating the homestead, milking the cattle, or selling the milk products. Women for their part do not participate in matters relating to the grazing, movement, or sale of cattle.

From about the age of puberty boys and girls begin to be prepared for their respective future roles as household heads and wives. Sexes are segregated in the camp

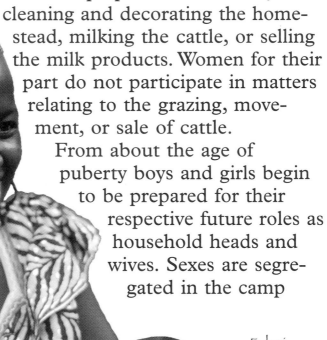

Fulani women are in charge of dairy products from the herds, household tasks, and childrearing.

as far as possible. For example, only household heads, infants, and females may sleep in the temporary shelters built by the Fulani. All other grown males sleep in the open around the cattle. Because of the nature and importance of gender roles, each household head aspires to have a fair balance of the sexes among his children. Sons are generally valued for continuing the family line, but all children, whether male or female, are equally welcome.

A strong link is made between the fertility of the family and that of the herd. It is believed, for instance, that the more sons and daughters a man has, the more likely it is for him to have a larger herd because of more efficient herding. The status of a household head is therefore enhanced by the size of the family and the herd.

▼ THE CLAN ▼

Next above the family unit is the clan, made up of households who trace their lineage back to a common male ancestor. The clan is a very loose unit, since the family units that make it up are rarely together. Occasionally clans may come together to form a camp comprising several unrelated households. A camp leader is elected on the basis of popularity linked to size of family and herd as well as maturity and wisdom. The camp leader has little real authority, however, since any family unit is free to leave the camp at

FULANI PROVERBS

Jalana qite bernde balejum kurum.
A laughing face and a black heart. (A person you can't trust.)

Bernde yidi dole terde jaggana nde.
The heart has desires, and the limbs act as its servants.

Mbuja humtata haje lingu.
Locust bean cakes will not keep the fish contented. (Not everybody has the same needs and likes.)

Ta gertogal wi'a u'an u'o ndau.
A fowl should not promise to squawk like an ostrich. (Never offer to do the impossible.)

Ko yali yarnge e hornge?
What does a cow that has just drunk care about a thirsty cow? (Most people worry only about their own well-being.)

Gikku didol tapare.
Personality is etched in stone.

Ta daru les lekki a tijja a fe'a lisal.
Never stand under the branch you're cutting down.

Wa'a jabbi nyo'a follere.
Climb the tamarind tree and shake down sorrel leaves. (Sometimes the unexpected happens.)

any time. Moreover, a leader's position lasts only as long as the camp exists.

The camp is useful for activities that require the participation of more than one family unit. A good example is marriage. The Fulani are basically endogamous; they tend to marry within the clan. The most preferred marriage is that between first cousins, sons and daughters of brothers and sisters. The camp affords an opportunity for this to be arranged.

The nomadic life is very lonely and harsh, as even the Fulani acknowledge. This is probably why they so much enjoy and look forward to the periods when they stay together in camp. Apart from the various social activities and ceremonies that can be held only in camps, the camp is also a rich source of information on matters concerning the well-being of the herd: weather and grazing, markets, and even political news that might help determine safe and unsafe areas.

▼ THE *SHARO* ▼

The institution of marriage is of vital importance to the nomadic Fulani, and all kinds of customs and ceremonies have arisen around it. One such ceremony is the *sharo*, a public flogging that is a test of manhood. Not all Fulani nomadic groups observe this ceremony or insist on it before a young man may marry. For some it is merely sport, indulged in for its own

A Fulani market. Marketplaces become places for Fulani festivals such as the *Sharo*.

sake. Probably the keenest exponents of the *sharo* are the Jafun Fulani found in Nigeria.

The *sharo* is a test of endurance; a youth is expected to undergo severe flogging in public without flinching. It is normally staged twice a year, during the dry-season guinea corn harvest and the Muslim festival of Id-el-kabir (called Sallan in Hausa). It may occasionally be held during a marriage, at the naming ceremony of the firstborn child of a renowned *sharo* exponent, to honor a chief, or as a contest between clans.

The *sharo* is a festival in its own right and attracts Fulani from far and near. It is usually held in a marketplace and lasts for a week. Men

and women gather at the marketplace all dressed
up for the occasion. Although various kinds of
entertainment are available—the maidens'
dance, performances by well-known minstrels,
and all kinds of tricksters—these are only a prel-
ude to the main act. The young men who are to
be flogged are attended by their seconds (those
who might act in their stead should they be unable to finish the act) and surrounded by a small
crowd of relatives, friends, and well-wishers.
When the *sharo* is about to begin, young men
carrying staffs and pretending fierceness clear
the ground of spectators. The tempo of the music, provided mainly by drums, quickens; the
youths cry shrilly and recite incantations.

At this point one of the young men to be
flogged comes out and strikes a defiant pose
with one leg crossed over the other and arms
raised clutching either a staff or a mirror into
which he gazes with apparent indifference. Another young man of about the same age and size
approaches, wielding a strong, supple cane
about a half inch thick, and moves around the
victim taking careful aim. Without warning he
lands the whip heavily on the other's ribs, sometimes drawing blood. Blow upon blow may be
struck, with the victim shouting for more. Other
youths acting as referees observe the proceedings
closely, ensuring that the blows are fairly struck.
The point, however, is that the victim does not

flinch but shows utter indifference to pain and even sneers at his attacker. If he is able to achieve this, his family and friends surround him with joy, offering gifts and congratulations. Even the belief that the youth may have fortified himself with charms and pain-resistant drugs does not dim the joy. He has now displayed his manhood and is considered worthy of a wife. Incidentally, the Fulani have herbal medicines that heal the wounds fairly quickly, leaving only scars that the youth may display for all to see.

▼ WOMEN'S LIFE ▼

Women do not undergo any initiation rite as dramatic as the *sharo*. They enjoy greater independence and freedom of movement than women of the surrounding Muslim populations. For example, although the Fulani have generally been Muslim for several centuries, they do not practice *purdah*, female seclusion in the home. The nomadic way of life would make this quite impossible. Women are segregated from men as far as circumstances allow and have clearly defined roles. No self-respecting man would dare interfere in the domestic roles reserved for women, such as the collection and disposal of dairy products. However, women have little direct voice in the political affairs of the community, nor can they aspire to roles of a political nature such as the leadership of a camp.

We have noted that the Fulani are polygynous, a man may marry more than one wife. Where there is more than one wife, the functions of the various wives are distributed evenly. The order of seniority is strictly maintained—a wife is senior to another depending on when she married rather than on her age. The most senior (or first) wife has clear authority over the others.

A woman has little choice in choosing a husband. Most marriages are arranged and in many cases are between cousins. When a girl is dissatis- fied with the choice of

Young Fulani women seldom have a say in whom they will marry.

Fulani elder and his wife seated on a beautiful mat.

husband, she has two options—to threaten sui-
cide or, in extreme cases, to run away from
home. The latter is a last resort because she
would probably end up in prostitution, thereby
bringing shame to her family. She may elope
with her preferred suitor.

If a marriage fails to work, divorce is relatively easy to obtain. Couples try to avoid divorce, however, since it brings shame to the man
and may leave the woman stranded. Thus, a
woman is not tied to an unhappy marriage, but
the alternative is poverty and perhaps prostitution if she does not remarry.

Women generally do not own cattle. When a
woman acquires cattle through inheritance or

marriage gifts, these are merged with her husband's and are counted as his. If the marriage breaks up, she has no access to her cattle, nor can she claim them when and if she remarries.

▼ DRESS AND DECORATION ▼

Pastoral Fulani women are noted for their distinctive and attractive dress and hairstyles. For both men and women, dress styles are influenced partly by what is available among the people with whom they live and partly by the demands of herding life.

In Hausaland, for instance, Fulani women wear simple bodycloths tied according to local custom, with elaborately designed short blouses for unmarried women. Long gowns are the vogue in Mali, whereas the very stylish dresses of Fulani women in Guinea and Senegal reflect the dress tastes of women in those areas.

In the desert areas clothes tend to be of dark hue; cloth turbans are worn by the men to keep out the dust, and women wear veils.

Men's dress tends to be less varied. Gowns are worn for attending market and ceremonial occasions. Their design ranges from the simple to the very elaborate. For purposes of herding, men wear shorter and purely functional tunics, and wide-brimmed straw hats.

Traditionally Fulani do not practice such

crafts as woodwork, leatherwork, or smithing.
Much of their innate artistry is invested in hairstyles and personal ornaments—mobile arts con-
nected to the body. There is great variety in
hairstyles. Hairdressing is begun at a very early
age, and plaiting, or braiding, is very popular. In
Hausaland the plaits tend to be simple in both
design and adornment. The favored style in
Niger is to have only two large plaits, joined
under the chin. In various places between Nigeria and Mali high crests of hair, sometimes
plaited, are built over cloth pads. Men plait their
hair as enthusiastically as women. They tend to
favor long plaits with less elaborate designs.
However, when a man marries he cuts off the
plaits and wears his hair short.

A good deal of care is given to the decoration
of the body. Plaits and hair crests may be deco-
rated with coins, amber beads, and even large
safety pins, artfully arranged. Necklaces are
adorned with the same kinds of materials. Earrings vary from place to place. They are of simple design in Benin Republic. In Nigeria sepa-
rate brass ornaments may hang from the rings.
In Niger, Burkina Faso, and Mali, Fulani
women may be practically weighed down by ear
decorations. Some wear as many as five rings in
each ear. Gold earrings are quite common.
Clusters of beads may decorate both ears and
neck.

Large gold earrings, such as those shown here, are worn by many Fulani women.

The Fulani have a wide variety of shelters because of the wide variations in living conditions. This settlement in Côte d'Ivoire has relatively permanent structures.

▼ SHELTERS ▼

The Fulani are less inventive and elaborate in the construction of their shelters, for the simple reason that shelters must be suited to nomadic life. Materials for construction depend on what is available. The roughest type of shelter, primarily a windbreak, is the cone-shaped dry-season shelter made of cornstalks. Sturdier shelters are made of plant branches fixed in the ground, bent over and tied in the center. This framework may be covered with smaller branches and leaves or date-palm fronds. The shelter may be thatched with grass or covered with mats. The huts are most often round. In Senegal, however, more elaborate, even T-shaped, dwellings are found, some 15 to 20 feet long.

Town Fulani, of course, build durable houses when they wish to do so. Their dwellings resemble those of the people among whom they live.

Living arrangements within the shelter vary from place to place. Basically the shelter is the preserve of the women—the men, including the household heads, are virtually guests. A woman spends much of her life in camp in the vicinity of the shelter. It is rare for shelters to be built when there are no women in camp.▲

chapter

4

WORLDVIEW, RELIGION, AND RITUALS

THE LIFE OF THE PASTORAL FULANI AND THEIR total outlook center on the maintenance of the family and the herd. The ultimate goal is the fulfillment of familial virtues—duties to elders, wives, and contemporaries that ensure the smooth working of the family and lineage group (or clan) as cooperating economic units. All these virtues are summed up in the notion of *pulaaku* or the "Fulani way." Certain general principles inform *pulaaku*.

The first is the principle of fertility, the continuity of the family line. Fertility ensures the supply of future herdsmen and milkmaids. An impotent man or a barren woman would find life extremely miserable for violating *pulaaku*, even if through no fault of their own. Impotent men resort to all sorts of devices to hide the fact, but barren women may be forced to abandon home and be driven into prostitution.

The second general principle is that of good husbandry, looking after the herd in a productive manner. Cattle should increase and multiply to provide for the next generation. Loss of cattle, whether through incompetence or disease, is deeply mourned. Fulani men enjoy attending markets, principally because they are the main source of news about weather, water supply, and epidemics. This helps to decide when and where to move their cattle in the most efficient manner.

The third general principle is the proper arrangement of children's marriages. Although this relates to the first principle of fertility, it has to do more with trying to ensure that the virtues and qualities of the clan are maintained. As we have seen, the preferred marriage is between first cousins—particularly the offspring of brothers. When this is not possible, marriage to less close relations is tolerated. Marriage outside the clan or into another ethnic group is discouraged.

One may also talk about certain basic components of *pulaaku* that derive from the general principles. The first component has to do with modesty and reserve, virtues that govern correct conduct in personal relations. This includes respect for elders and seniors. Great respect is given to age, and the views of experienced elders are never dismissed lightly. Respect for seniority pervades Fulani life. Siblings are ranked by age. The eldest son, for example, has authority over his younger siblings and priority in inheritance. The household heads in a camp are also arranged in order of seniority. Although a camp leader is elected, the elder of widest experience and wisdom is regarded as the guardian of the Fulani way and may impose sanctions for violations of *pulaaku*.

Another aspect of the component of modesty and reserve is cooperation with peers. When social activities bring the Fulani together, everyone is expected to cooperate. Cooperation is even more vital with regard to looking after the herd. When families camp together, they take turns in looking after the herd or performing camp duties. This frees others to attend markets. If loss of cattle is suffered, stock may be replenished through loans or outright gifts.

Another aspect of modesty and reserve is the avoidance of certain kinsfolk under potentially hostile situations. The Fulani go to extraordinary lengths to avoid situations that have a potential for embarrassment or hostility in dealing with kinfolk. It is better to flee than to lose face.

A second basic component of *pulaaku* has to do with patience and fortitude. It is recognized that life is hard and that strength lies in withstanding adversity. Fortitude must be shown in times of bereavement; one is not expected to

Today the majority of Fulani, particularly the settled Fulani, are Muslim, like this man wearing a Muslim fez.

break down in grief. A man must also be patient in dealing with wives and children. A polygynous household is not easy to manage. A man must strive to balance the competing demands of wives and children while maintaining peace and harmony.

Patience and fortitude must also be shown in time of cattle disease epidemics. When nothing can be done, one should bear the loss, which amounts to bereavement in its own right. Probably the most trying period in the life of a herdsman is the height of the dry season. Patience and fortitude must be evident during this time of hardship while searching for water and grazing land. It is a time when pastoral Fulani can become involved in clashes with owners of the land through which the cattle pass.

The third basic component of *pulaaku* relates to care and forethought. This refers to the duties that belong to the Fulani. For example, a herdsman should inspect his cattle carefully every morning before they leave the corral. He should light a fire at dusk when the cattle return, in obedience to the water spirit that gave Fulani cattle. The fire must be put out every morning when the cattle leave the corral. A herdsman must attend market for the purpose of gathering intelligence necessary for the efficient movement of his cattle. Finally, he should show respect to constituted authority, such as village and district heads placed over him by the will of Allah, the Muslim God. If this is not possible, it is better to flee than to risk confrontation.

A man who habitually flouts the *pulaaku* code is regarded as mad. No sane man would risk severing himself physically and morally from the rest of the community, which is the accepted consequence of violating the code. For example, when a man breaches the code seriously, he may be required by the guardian of the code to live in isolation in the bush for some time. Small quantities of milk are sent to him twice a day. He neither washes nor shaves his hair and looks like an animal. This is considered appropriate because he has, through his conduct, taken himself out of the human race. He is readmitted to society when he shows sufficient repentance.

▼ ISLAM VS. TRADITION ▼

The Fulani came into contact with Islam probably as far back as the 7th century AD. The faith spread quickly among many of the settled and nomadic populations. Although there are pockets of nonbelievers who still engage only in traditional religious practices, the Fulani are predominantly Muslim.

Elements of traditional religious practices have survived, however. We have mentioned the belief in water spirits. Among the Fulani are men who know herbal healing practices, divination, and even magic. Nomads are faced with dangers and experiences not covered by the Islamic holy book, the Koran, and they have traditional ways of dealing with them. In many cases these traditional practices and beliefs have been blended with Islamic teaching, and it is not easy to disentangle them.

Some religious practices that probably have their origin in pre-Islamic times still exist. Some of these are taken from fertility rites, others from rites of passage. All of them relate to the spiritual and moral well-being of the community. For example, in the wet season, livestock contests are held at which prize beasts are paraded and judged. This is no mere award-winning contest. It is a solemn occasion presided over by the guardian of *pulaaku* and may be interpreted as a celebration of the productivity of the herd. The greater the number of prize beasts displayed, the more successful the occasion is considered to be.

Another occasion is the herd owner's feast, at which a bull that has served ten seasons is presented to his clansfolk for one of the rare meat feasts indulged in by the Fulani. Again, the point is not the meat, but the symbolic consumption of a fertile bull believed to possess a quality that is highly valued and hoped for in family and herd.

Even more interesting but of less clear significance is the *gerewol* contest, a dance of youths before elders. Young men dress in finery: ostrich-feather caps, leather belts trimmed with cowrie shells, ceremonial axes. They dance a slow, stamping rhythm while praising in song the charms of the young women. These young women are graded in order of beauty. No drum-ming accompanies the dance. Meanwhile the young women dance nearby, choosing also by way of song the most handsome and best-dressed youths. The "best" three or four young men and women are paired off in that order, while the rest pair off as they will. Each couple is expected to spend the evening together. Al-though a recognized form of courtship, the *gerewol* dance does not necessarily lead to mar-riage. One can only presume that this ceremo-nial dance and its aftermath are survivals of an early fertility rite.

Other important events include the naming ceremony, male circumcision, and *sharo*. The naming ceremony and male circumcision prob-ably have an Islamic origin, since they exist in other Islamic communities. Every newborn child is named on the seventh day of its life at a cer-emony normally presided over by an Islamic scholar. The naming of the firstborn child, male or female, has special significance and is often accompanied by fasting.

Every male child must be circumcised at the

Few Town Fulani, such as this young man, continue to follow pre-Islamic traditions.

age of nine or ten. Unlike the naming ceremony, no special activity is associated with this occasion. It is meant to mark the end of puberty and the introduction of the initiate into young adulthood and the added responsibility of looking after the herd.

These traditions are meant to ensure that the functions of the family and lineage are fulfilled and its norms of conduct enforced and perpetuated as values. Few of these practices are now observed by the Town Fulani, representing what may be described as a cultural difference between the settled and nomadic Fulani. But as we shall see in the next chapter, when it came to establishing military, political, and Islamic dominance in parts of West Africa, and the building of empires, there was unity of purpose between the two groups.

5

MILITARY, POLITICAL, AND ISLAMIC DOMINANCE

BETWEEN THE 10TH AND 18TH CENTURIES, THE Fulani established at least seven different kingdoms and empires in various parts of West Africa. The later states, better known because they were encountered by European colonizers, were clearly inspired by the need to spread Islam. It is easy, therefore, to forget that Fulani empire-building did not always have a religious basis. Other social and economic factors also came into play.

Non-Islamic Fulani states were founded in Fouta Jalon in the 10th century and in Fouta Toro in the 1500s. The latter state was established by the Fulani Denianke clan, who had fled to Senegal from oppressive rule in Songhay, one of the famous empires of West Africa. Other states founded in this period by non-Islamic

Fulani dynasties were in Gobir (Nigeria), Macina (Mali), and Bagirmi. The Fulani rulers of these states persecuted Muslim populations under their rule when they thought it necessary for maintaining power.

▼ EMPIRE–BUILDING ▼

After this phase came the period when the Fulani either created or seized already existing Muslim states. Within a single century they controlled so many states in West Africa that it appeared they would unite the whole region under one ruler. But that was not to be.

The first Muslim state was Fouta Jalon. In 1725, Alfa Ba, a Muslim Fulani, put himself at the head of a coalition of the many Fulani pastoralists who had migrated to this highland area. He declared a *jihad* on the non-Islamic Fulani ruling dynasty of Fouta Jalon and the largely non-Muslim Sosso and Mandingo inhabitants of the area. Alfa Ba died while still preparing for war, but his son, Karamoko Alfa, carried on his father's plans with the help of a war leader known as Ibrahim Sori. Together they conquered almost the entire state of Fouta Jalon and put in place an administrative system that survives today in modified form.

The second Muslim Fulani state was also imposed on an existing state ruled by a non-Muslim Fulani dynasty. This was at Fouta Toro.

Abdulkadir Torodi, a Muslim Fulani holy man, led the minority Muslim Fulani in rebellion against the Denianke rulers, whom he defeated. He was able to hold the state together until his death in 1788. His style of administration split the area into provinces, each governed by a holy man. His was therefore a clear theocracy, which continued to expand through war until the arrival of the French in the 18th century.

The next Muslim Fulani state was imposed on the existing kingdom of Macina. The Fulani had long been unhappy subjects of the ruling Bamana, another West African people. This ended when a Fulani Muslim, Ahmadu Sisi, led a successful uprising and proclaimed himself Emir of Macina. His reign was marked by fierce fanaticism. He did not hesitate to persecute those Muslims whom he felt to be less than devoted to their faith.

By far the most significant attempt at empire-building was that undertaken by another Fulani holy man, Usuman Dan Fodio, in what is now northern Nigeria. He created a substantial empire, defeating and taking over many of the existing Hausa kingdoms and founding new kingdoms of his own. Dan Fodio was born in Degel in the Hausa kingdom of Gobir, northwest of Sokoto in Nigeria. He was brought up a strict Muslim of the Maliki sect and realized early that he had a talent for writing and especially preaching. It was through his preaching that he began his empire-building career. Like the other Fulani holy men turned empire-builders, he started by criticizing severely the relaxed Islamic practices of the rulers. He accused the Hausa rulers specifically of mixing "pagan" with Islamic practices. This irritated the Gobir rulers, Nafata and later his son, Yunfa, both of whom incidentally had been former pupils of Dan Fodio.

Yunfa caused Dan Fodio to flee Degel in February, 1804. Dan Fodio retired to a remote part of the kingdom, from where he sent messages calling for support from Fulani communities. These responded in considerable numbers, including many pastoral Fulani. Dan Fodio declared a *jihad* on Yunfa and with his band of fervent believers met and defeated Yunfa at the battle of Kwotto Lake in 1804.

Dan Fodio was proclaimed commander of the faithful by his victorious army and took the title of *Shehu* or *Sheik*. He extended his holy war to all enemies of Islam, and within ten years he and his son Bello, who later succeeded him, had taken several existing kingdoms or carved out new ones either through insurrection or war. By 1810 the Hausa states of Katsina, Kano, Zaria, and Daura had been overcome. Dan Fodio modeled his empire after the Caliphs (or rulers) who succeeded the Prophet Muhammad, and he set up headquarters of his Caliphate (ruling class) in the city of Sokoto, which had recently been built. He retired to a life of contemplation, leaving the process of expansion of the empire in the able hands of his son Bello and Dan Fodio's younger brother, Abdullahi.

Within the next 20 years, old states such as Nupe and Ilorin were taken over, and new states such as Adamawa, Bauchi, Hadejia, and Katagun were established. When the British arrived late in the 19th century, these states had been so well established that the British chose to base their rule on the existing administrative system. Many of the present Emirs of these states are descended from Dan Fodio's original flagbearers.

The Fulani had, over a period of about eight centuries, established themselves as a political and military force over large portions of West Africa. Some speculate that but for the arrival of the British, French, and German colonizers, the Fulani would have greatly extended their control over the surrounding territory. Others dispute this because the grassland savanna over which the Fulani operated so effectively with their cavalry was radically different from the dense forests to be found toward the coastal areas. It is practically impossible to maneuver cavalry effectively in thick forest, and this would have limited Fulani expansion.

COLONIALISM AND THE FULANI

The Fulani's colonial history is more complicated than that of some other peoples, because the Fulani have long been spread out over many countries in West Africa. Although they were technically one empire, the Fulani were too widely dispersed to be able to communicate well and work as a unit to defend their empire. As they faced violent threats from the Germans, French, and British in the late 1700s, each segment of the empire had to work on its own behalf. In addition, sometimes even neighboring regions of the Fulani empire were unable to cooperate because of quarrels and grudges among the aristocracy or hostilities between Muslims and Christians.

The Fulani's defense potential was further weakened by the fact that, as a powerful empire, they were constantly at odds with their neighbors. To build the empire they had subdued many other peoples, and to keep the empire together they forced those conquered peoples to pay them tribute or serve them in other ways, causing much ill feeling. In times of trouble, especially against powerful European enemies, it was always tempting for the Fulani's subjects to join with the invading forces if they thought there was a chance of regaining their independence.

In attempts to defend their kingdom from the European invaders, the Fulani problem was not lack of troops. One of the largest Fulani armies, in the city of Tibati in Cameroon, had 10,000 infantry and 3,000 horsemen. They did not, however, have many modern weapons. Ten thousand of the finest archers and swordsmen in Africa were no match for a few hundred German soldiers with cannons and rifles. Germany took over Tibati in 1899, greatly demoralizing Fulani all over the empire.

In 1900, Britain announced that all of the Fulani emirates in Nigeria would come under British rule. Zubeiru, the leader in the city of Yola in the Adamawa Highlands, was an example of a ruler who would not bow to the British. Zubeiru worked bravely to organize his people and stand up against the invasion. He even had two cannons and a few hundred rifles. Although his own troops were not trained to use these weapons, he did find some immigrants to the Fulani kindom who were willing to fight for him and teach others.

The British in Nigeria were more scheming and determined than Zubeiru imagined, however. Knowing that Zubeiru would fight fiercely, they had been sending urgent messages to the British Parliament asking for more troops. They made up stories about Zubeiru, claiming that he was mad and violent and a threat to the British in the area. Their plan worked, and the British government sent more soldiers and weapons than the forces at Yola could grapple with.

Whenever the French, Germans, or British conquered an area, their first move was to depose the current Fulani ruler and replace him with someone willing to be loyal to the colonial government. The British actually tried to persuade Zubeiru to work as a loyalist leader in Yola, thinking that they could profit from his regional influence in trade agreements. Zubeiru refused to be anyone's puppet, however, and instead exiled himself from his homeland.

All of Fulani territory was under European rule by the early years of the 20th century. Germany gained control of Cameroon's valuable coastal region in 1884. After World War II the French took over most of the land, leaving a small concession to the British. Niger was conquered by France in 1897. Nigeria was badgered by the British for decades before their official takeover in 1903. Gambia, too, was a British colony, while the French beat out the Portuguese and British for control of Senegal in 1895.

The years following World War II brought universal unrest to the African subjects of colonial rule. Brilliant political leaders such as Léopold Sédar Senghor of Niger led West African peoples to unite against the imposed foreign governments. Niger, Cameroon, Nigeria, Senegal, and Gambia all proclaimed their independence in 1960.

One clear outcome of the Fulani holy wars of the 18th and 19th centuries was the Islamization of large segments of the West African population and the establishment of Islamic domination over much of the area. Some would even talk of a "Fulani phase of Islamization" because many of the leaders of the empire-building ventures were Islamic holy men anxious to propagate some "pure" form of their faith. But it must be remembered that in many cases the usurped states were already Islamic, though not satisfactorily strict in the eyes of the *jihad* leaders. There is no doubt, however, that they transformed western Africa religiously and politically to an extent matched only by the later Christianization of the area by European interests.

▼ EFFECTS OF THE *JIHADS* ▼

The *jihads* also had social and economic consequences. They opened up vast areas to commerce, especially to traveling Hausa traders, and facilitated the intermingling of previously isolated and hostile peoples, giving them a new sense of identity and raising their political consciousness. An intellectual renaissance was brought about by the revival of Islamic learning in the tradition of Timbuktu, the great and ancient center of learning.

The Fulani were spectacularly successful

Trade has always been an important feature of Fulani life; even holy men engaged in it. The sale of spices at markets such as this has been going on for centuries.

in their empire-building efforts, despite the fact that they constituted a minority population wherever they lived and were widely dispersed.

The role of the so-called holy men of the period cannot be underestimated. A holy man was a man sanctified. Ultimately his sanctification derived from Allah through his prophets. A holy man lived on fees obtained by performing special tasks such as the preparation of charms and amulets, and divination. He could also farm, engage in trade, or practice a craft, but he was essentially a teacher and a preacher. To give to him was equivalent to the giving of alms, one of the basic pillars, or duties, of Islam.

Holy men of this type seem to have been a peculiarly West African phenomenon. They have been described as the "spearhead" of Islam in the region. Some holy men had little learning, whereas others such as Dan Fodio acquired international reputations as scholars. These holy men were able to convert princes, introduce administrative reforms, and, when displeased, lead insurrections against the rulers. They were almost always of settled Fulani stock, but their message attracted both pastoralists and sedentary nonbelievers. They did not hesitate to hire mercenary soldiers and "unbelievers" when it suited them. The uprisings against governments were usually marked initially more by religious fervor than by clear military strategy. But the holy men tended to learn fast.

Another reason for the Fulani successes was their efficient military organization. Their soldiers were well armed by the standards of the times, making use of bows, spears, swords, quilted armor, chain mail, and later guns. Although their foot soldiers acquitted themselves well in battle, their great secret lay in the imaginative use of heavy cavalry. Covered by showers of arrows fired by the foot soldiers, the cavalry

Fulani populations, particularly nomadic ones, are faced with difficult choices between their traditions and government policies. In Niger the government has forced nomads to carry identity cards and encourages them to settle. In Central African Republic, where these Fulani live, their need for grazing conflicts with wildlife preservation, and armed officials drive the Bororo away.

operated as shock troops, driving fear into and demoralizing their enemies. In short, the Fulani dominance lay in their intelligent use of superior arms and tactics.

Finally, the Fulani succeeded in imposing, by a combination of military force and diplomacy, a single government over a large heterogeneous area. They introduced the idea of constructing an Islamic state modeled on the early Islamic rule, the caliphate. They promoted intellectual growth through the revival of Islamic learning, and they stimulated commerce and the development of trade over almost all of the West African region.▲

6

THE FUTURE

THE FULANI HAVE UNDOUBTEDLY MADE significant contributions to the history and development of the West African region. They continue to do so at present and will continue to do so in future. It is not easy to talk about the future of so complex and widespread a people.

The future of the settled Fulani is intimately linked with that of the various communities among whom they live. With them, they are experiencing all the pangs (and joys) of modernization. Quite a number of them have distinguished themselves in various areas of endeavor and occupy leadership positions in several countries.

Things are not so straightforward for the pastoral Fulani. The nomadic life is becoming difficult because more and more land is being taken over for agriculture and other purposes. The main problem then is the conservation and efficient management of grazing land. As the Fulani remain by far the major suppliers of cattle and thus the main source of meat in the area, the problem cannot be underestimated. The various governments have been seeking ways to tackle the problem as well as trying to reduce the friction that it sometimes causes between the nomadic Fulani and the farmers.

The pastoral Fulani are not in a hurry to abandon the nomadic life or their age-old and time-tested way of doing things. Attempts to confine them to ranches and other such facilities have not been successful. There have also been efforts to integrate their cattle-raising ways with the demands of modern life. A good example is the nomadic education program being carried out in Nigeria whereby nomadic Fulani children are provided with modern educational facilities without disrupting their way of life.

Nomads are under great pressure to change or modify their way of life. One of the main reasons is because nomads cross national frontiers, making it very difficult for the countries Fulani travel through to administer them. It will be interesting to see how things turn out in future.▲

Glossary

Bororo "Cattle Fulani" who live a nomadic existence.

Caliph Muslim ruler.

Fulfulde The language of the Fulani.

gerewol Ceremonial courtship dance by young men and women before the elders.

Hegira The flight of the prophet Muhammad from Medina.

heterogeneous Having a foreign origin.

holy men Muslim scholars and missionaries.

jihad Holy war.

pulaaku "The Fulani Way" of familial virtues.

purdah Seclusion of women, practiced in Islamic communities.

sharo Ceremonial public flogging of young men, practiced as a ritual and a sport.

Toroobo "Town Fulani," agriculturists who live in settled communities.

rite of passage Ceremony marking a change in life status.

theocracy Government of a state by divine influence or guidance.

For Further Reading

Boyd, Jean. *The Flame of Islam: A Simple Account of the Fulani Jihad in Sokoto.* Zaria: Northern Nigerian Pub. Co., 1969.

Chesi, Gert. *The Last Africans.* Worgl, Austria: Perlinger, 1977.

Milsome, John. *Usuman Dan Fodio: Great Leader and Reformer.* Ibadan: Oxford University Press, 1968.

Whitting, Charles Edward Jewel. *Hausa and Fulani Proverbs.* Farnborough, Hampshire: Gregg Press, 1967.

Challenging Reading

Hopen, C. E. *The Pastoral Fulbe Family of Gwandu.* London: Oxford University Press, 1958.

Johnston, Hugh A. S. *The Fulani Empire of Sokoto.* London/Ibadan: Oxford University Press, 1967.

Maddox, Gregory. *Conquest and Resistance to Colonialism in Africa.* New York: Garland, 1993.

Stenning, D. J. *Savannah Nomads.* London: Oxford University Press, 1959.

Film

Adama, The Fulani Magician (motion picture). Jim Rosellini for African Family Films.

Index

ABOUT THE AUTHOR
Pat Ikechukwu Ndukwe holds a B.A. degree from the University of Ife, Nigeria, and a Ph.D. from the University of York, England. He teaches linguistics at the University of Nigeria, Nsukka, with a specialization in Sociolinguistics and Language Planning. With a keen interest in Nigerian languages and cultures, he has researched the Igbo, Kanuri, and Fulani. He has also published articles in local and international journals.

COMMISSIONING EDITOR: Chukwuma Azuonye, Ph.D.

CONSULTING EDITOR: Gary N. Van Wyk, Ph.D.

PHOTO CREDITS: Cover, pp. 8, 17, 23, 32, 36, 46 © Phyllis Galembo; p. 10 (top) © Chris Caldecott/Royal Geographical Society; pp. 10 (bottom), 13, 14, 20 (top), 20 (bottom), 56 © Katie Arkell/Gamma Liaison; pp. 24, 28, 31, 35, 41 © Herbert M. Cole; p. 55 © Peter Holmes/Royal Geographical Society.

DESIGN: Kim Sonsky.